CREW

...l hurricanes are frightening. They begin out at sea ...d quickly build up into a huge heat engine, bigger and ...onger than a thousand bombs. They bring rain and ...ods and savage, violent winds, which can break a ...an's neck. Nobody can stop a hurricane. You can ...ly wait and watch, and hope to God it never comes ...ar you.

...rricane Mabel is going to be very nasty indeed. ...vid Wyatt, a young weather scientist, has a strange ...ling about Mabel. She should stay out at sea and not ...me near the Caribbean island of San Fernandez. But ...yatt believes she will change direction and hit the ...nd. He can't explain why – he just knows he is right.

...ile Mabel moves slowly northwards, some people ...San Fernandez are worrying about another danger – ...r, which also brings death. War seems more ...portant to them. They can fight a war, and win. But ...ey can't fight a hurricane, so they should listen to ...yatt . . . before it is too late.

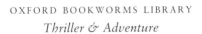

OXFORD BOOKWORMS LIBRARY
Thriller & Adventure

Wyatt's Hurricane

Stage 3 (1000 headwords)

Series Editor: Jennifer Bassett
Founder Editor: Tricia Hedge
Activities Editors: Jennifer Bassett and Alison Baxter

DESMOND BAGLEY

Wyatt's Hurricane

Retold by
Jennifer Bassett

OXFORD UNIVERSITY PRESS

OXFORD

UNIVERSITY PRESS

Great Clarendon Street, Oxford OX2 6DP

Oxford University Press is a department of the University of Oxford.
It furthers the University's objective of excellence in research, scholarship,
and education by publishing worldwide in

Oxford New York

Auckland Cape Town Dar es Salaam Hong Kong Karachi
Kuala Lumpur Madrid Melbourne Mexico City Nairobi
New Delhi Shanghai Taipei Toronto

With offices in

Argentina Austria Brazil Chile Czech Republic France Greece
Guatemala Hungary Italy Japan Poland Portugal Singapore
South Korea Switzerland Thailand Turkey Ukraine Vietnam

OXFORD and OXFORD ENGLISH are registered trade marks of
Oxford University Press in the UK and in certain other countries

Original edition © 1966 by Desmond Bagley
First published 1966 by William Collins & Co Ltd
This simplified edition © Oxford University Press 2008

Database right Oxford University Press (maker)

First published in Oxford Bookworms 1992

2 4 6 8 10 9 7 5 3 1

Any websites referred to in this publication are in the public domain and
their addresses are provided by Oxford University Press for information only.
Oxford University Press disclaims any responsibility for the content

ISBN 978 0 19 479138 0

Printed in Hong Kong

Illustrated by: Simon Anderson/The Organisation

Word count (main text): 10,500 words

For more information on the Oxford Bookworms Library,
visit www.oup.com/elt/bookworms

CONTENTS

1
Flying into the hurricane

The silver aeroplane flew south-east in fair weather, across the small green islands called the Lesser Antilles. The sky above was clear, and the blue Atlantic below shone in the bright sunshine. But somewhere, far out above the Atlantic, trouble was waiting and the plane flew on to look for it.

The pilot, Harry Hansen, was an officer in the United States Navy, with twelve years' flying behind him. He stared hard at the sky in front of him, and at last saw the first thin clouds appear. He pushed a button and spoke into the radio.

'We're getting near, Dave. Any change of orders?'

Officers in the United States Navy didn't usually take orders from a foreigner, but that didn't worry Hansen. He was a sensible man. He liked to fly with men who were good at their jobs – and who would help him to get the plane back home in one piece.

David Wyatt came forward to speak to Hansen and looked out at the sky. Already the clouds were thicker and heavier. In a few more minutes the plane would be in the storm.

'We'll take the usual route in,' he said. 'We'll follow the wind round in a circle, moving slowly inwards all the time. When we get to the south-west corner, we'll turn into the centre.'

'OK,' said Hansen. 'But I hope you get all the information that you need. I don't want to do this twice.'

Wyatt smiled. 'Neither do I.'

He went back down the plane and fastened himself into his seat. The two men who worked with him were already busy. The three of them made sure that everything was safe and that nothing could move. They checked that the instruments were working and the computers were ready.

Wyatt was frightened. He was always frightened just before the plane went in, because he knew more about hurricanes than any man on the plane. Hurricanes were his job, his life study, and he understood too well the danger of flying into those terrible, violent winds.

The clouds were now black mountains hundreds of metres high. Gently, Hansen began to turn the plane deeper into the storm. The winds became more and more violent and the plane shook from nose to tail. Rain drove upwards through the clouds and lightning filled the sky with a hard blue light.

Suddenly the plane dropped like a stone. Hansen fought against the wind and pushed the plane into a climb. All around, the blue-black clouds were exploding into different shapes every second. Then, just as suddenly, another wind hit the plane from below, and the plane shot upwards like a bullet from a gun.

Hansen's arms ached as he fought the plane. He took a quick look at his watch. Another half an hour before he could turn towards the centre, and then another 160 kilometres through the crosswinds before they reached it.

In the back of the plane, Wyatt and his men were very busy. Although they were beaten and shaken every second by the plane's violent movements, they still managed to do their work.

At last the plane flew into the 'eye' of the hurricane – that strange place of calm, peaceful air in the centre of the storm.

'How are you doing back there, Dave?' came Hansen's voice over the radio.

'Not too bad,' replied Wyatt. 'More than half of the

Hansen's arms ached as he fought the plane.

instruments are still working. I think we'll get most of the information that we need.'

'This is a really bad storm, Dave. I'll give you five minutes, then we're flying out again. It's going to be worse on the way out.'

And it was. For more than an hour the winds screamed and beat against the plane, and tried to break it into pieces. Wyatt was afraid that the wings would come off, but at last they reached calm air again and the noise of the hurricane died away behind them.

Four hours later they were back on the ground at Cap Sarrat. As they left the plane, Hansen turned to Wyatt.

'If I have to fly through another storm like that, I'm going to take a ground job.'

Wyatt laughed. 'Well, that was the worst one that I've ever seen. And I've flown into twenty-three hurricanes.'

'Twenty-three!' Hansen shook his head. 'You must be crazy!'

*　*　*　*　*

Back at his desk the next morning, Wyatt began to work on the information about the hurricane. His office was in the US Navy Base at Cap Sarrat on the island of San Fernandez. From his window Wyatt could look out across the blue waters of Santego Bay towards St Pierre, the capital of the island. It was a beautiful picture, bright and clear in the hot West Indian sun.

But this morning Wyatt had no time to look out of the window. Although he was young, still in his twenties, he was a good weather scientist and knew his job well. He did not like hurricanes, and this new hurricane he did not like at all. When

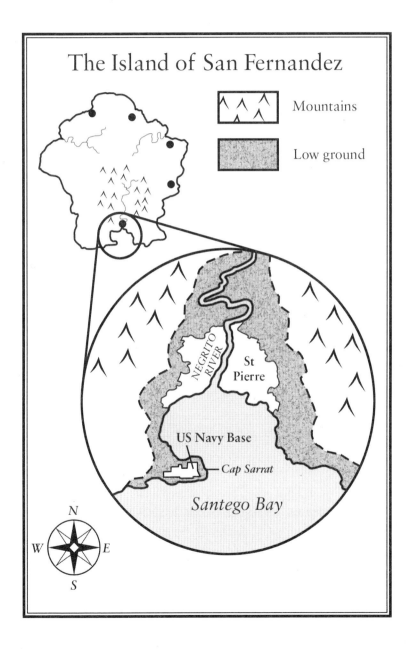

The Island of San Fernandez

Mountains

Low ground

NEGRITO RIVER

St Pierre

US Navy Base

Cap Sarrat

Santego Bay

N
W E
S

he had finished adding up all his figures, he studied the map carefully. Then he went to see Schelling, the US officer who was the chief weather scientist at the Base.

'This hurricane is going to be a bad one,' Wyatt told him. 'Look at these figures. The winds could be up to 270 kilometres an hour.'

Schelling studied the figures. 'Mmm. Not very nice,' he agreed. 'What's the name of this one?'

Wyatt looked through his papers. 'Let me see – H, I, J, K, L ... The last one was Laura, so this one will be Mabel. She's moving slowly northwards at the moment, but she could change direction and come our way. I think we should—'

'Oh, I don't think she will,' said Schelling quickly. 'If we look at examples of other hurricanes, the direction will very probably stay north. Mabel will finish somewhere out in the North Atlantic and not reach land at all. I think we can safely tell the Weather Office that.'

'I don't agree!' Wyatt said angrily. 'We just don't know enough about hurricanes and how they change direction. Look at Isobel in 1955 – she changed direction seven times in ten days, and ended up right in the mouth of the St Lawrence river in Canada!'

They argued for a while longer, but Schelling had very fixed ideas and would not accept that facts and figures did not always give a true picture. Wyatt returned unhappily to his office. In one way, Schelling was right. At the moment there was no real reason to think that Mabel *would* change direction. But reason wasn't everything. Wyatt just had a feeling about Mabel – a very strong feeling in the bottom of his stomach. He started to work through his figures again, looking for something to explain his fear.

Suddenly the phone rang, and when Wyatt answered it, he forgot all about Mabel.

'Julie!' he said. 'Fantastic! Where are you?' He heard the warm laugh that he remembered so well, and his heart jumped inside him. A few minutes later he had agreed to meet her that evening in the one hotel in St Pierre.

Julie Marlowe, he thought in surprise. She worked for a travel company, and she and Wyatt had been very friendly for a while. Then her company moved her to the United States and Wyatt had not seen her for a year. But he had not forgotten her. What was she doing back in St Pierre? Had she come to see him? Wyatt began to hope.

—— 2 ——
A night out in St Pierre

W yatt did not find the answer to his questions that evening. Julie seemed very pleased to see him, but did not seem to want to be alone with him. When he went into the bar of the Grand Hotel, she was talking to an older man with short grey hair and a square face. Julie introduced him as John Causton, an Englishman who was a newspaper reporter with a big London paper. Then a few minutes later Harry Hansen came in and joined them, and the four of them stayed together all evening. Wyatt was very cross about that, but there was nothing that he could do about it.

Causton was very interested in Wyatt. 'Why is an Englishman working for the United States Navy?' he asked.

'I'm not English. I'm a West Indian,' explained Wyatt. 'My family has been in the West Indies for nearly four hundred years. And I don't work *for* the Navy, I work *with* them. They've borrowed me from the Weather Office, and I'm doing a special study on hurricanes.'

'What's the latest news on Mabel?' asked Hansen.

Wyatt looked unhappy. 'I'm worried about her,' he said. 'I've got a strange feeling that she's going to do something unusual, but I don't know what or when.'

'She's a bad girl, all right,' said Hansen.

'And who', said Julie coldly, 'is Mabel?'

Hansen laughed. 'One of Dave's girls. He's got a lot of them. Remember Laura a few months ago, Dave? You had some fun with her!'

'And so did you!' said Wyatt, smiling.

Causton suddenly laughed. 'You're talking about hurricanes, aren't you?'

Julie smiled, but said crossly, 'Why must they give girls' names to hurricanes? Why not men's names?'

'Girls' names are easy to remember,' said Wyatt, with a serious face, 'and so hard to forget.' He smiled at her suddenly, and Julie's face went a little pink. Wyatt began to feel more hopeful. While Causton and Hansen went to buy more drinks, he asked Julie to spend the next afternoon with him. She agreed readily, and Wyatt began to feel that the evening was a success after all.

During dinner in the restaurant, Julie asked Wyatt to explain why hurricanes happened.

Hansen laughed. 'Don't start him talking about hurricanes. He'll go on for hours!'

Causton took out his notebook. 'I'm a newspaperman,' he said, smiling. 'I'm always interested in information.'

'Well,' began Wyatt. 'First, you need a warm sea and still air. The warm air just above the sea rises, wet and heavy, and cooler air comes in from the sides underneath to take its place. Then, because the world is turning, this moving air also begins to turn.' He borrowed Causton's notebook and began to draw pictures to show them. 'Higher up, the warm wet air meets cold air, and the water in the warm air starts to fall as rain. This also makes a lot of heat, and so everything begins to get hotter and bigger, and move faster. The winds are now moving in a circle and pulling outwards, so the air pressure in the centre of the circle becomes very low. This is the "eye" of the hurricane, where the air is very still. But the air pressure on the outside of the circle is very high, so the winds move faster and faster to try to get into the centre. And so a hurricane is born. Then it begins to move forward, and meets more warm sea and still air, and everything is repeated. A hurricane is a huge heat engine, bigger and stronger than a thousand bombs.'

Wyatt stopped, and Julie looked at him. 'Well, I hope Mabel doesn't come near San Fernandez,' she said.

'When did you last have a hurricane here?' asked Causton.

'In 1910. It hit St Pierre and killed 6,000 people.'

'1910? Perhaps we shouldn't worry about Mabel, then,' said Causton. 'And I've heard that there are other dangers here. President Serrurier, for example. I've heard that he's killed 20,000 people on this island since he's been President.'

Hansen shook his head. 'Serrurier is bad news,' he said, 'but nobody can stop him.'

They finished their meal and moved back into the hotel bar.

Causton bought them all drinks, and then asked,

'Have any of you heard of a man called Favel?'

'Julio Favel?' said Wyatt. 'Yes. He's dead.'

'Serrurier's men caught him in the hills last year and killed him. That was the story in the newspapers here,' said Hansen. He turned to Julie and explained, 'Favel was a rebel, but he was very popular with the people here. They wanted him to fight Serrurier and win, and so become the new President.'

Causton picked up his glass. 'I've heard,' he said lazily, 'that Favel is still alive.'

Wyatt looked at him and smiled. He decided that he liked John Causton. 'Ah!' he said. 'So that's why you've come to San Fernandez. Where there's a newsman, there's always trouble.'

'I think it's the other way round,' said Causton gently. 'Where there's trouble, there's always a newsman.'

The conversation turned to other things, and not long afterwards Wyatt and Hansen left to return to the Base. As they drove through St Pierre, they noticed a lot of police standing at street corners. There were also large groups of soldiers marching through the streets.

'Serrurier must be worried about something,' said Wyatt. 'Perhaps Causton's right about Favel.'

'If it *is* true that Favel's alive,' said Hansen unhappily, 'there's going to be a lot of trouble.'

Outside the town, the road to Cap Sarrat was quiet. All the way home Wyatt thought about Julie, and about her smile, and what she had said, and what she hadn't said.

He also thought a little about Mabel.

'I've heard,' said Causton, 'that Favel is still alive.'

— 3 —
'The big wind is coming'

The next morning more information came in about Mabel. Satellite photographs showed that she was now 900 kilometres south-east of San Fernandez and the other islands. She was moving a little faster now, in a north-eastern direction. Wyatt studied the information carefully. There was still no reason why Mabel should change direction towards San Fernandez. But Wyatt still had this strange feeling in his stomach. Mabel was trouble. She was getting stronger all the time. Her winds were too fast, the air pressure in her 'eye' was too low. A small change in her direction could mean thousands of deaths.

At lunchtime Wyatt put away his papers and maps, and went to meet Julie. They drove up into the mountains behind St Pierre, past fields full of fruit trees, where the island people worked fourteen hours a day, seven days a week.

Julie stared out of the window. 'They look so poor,' she said.

'They *are* poor,' said Wyatt. 'Serrurier owns most of the land, and he pays the workers almost nothing. The money from the fruit farms is spent on guns and bombs for the soldiers, not on schools and hospitals for the people.'

'Why do you stay here?' asked Julie. 'Couldn't you move to the States and do your study on hurricanes there?'

'I'm doing my best work here,' said Wyatt. 'And I'm a West Indian. This is my home.'

He drove for several kilometres and then stopped. They got out of the car, and looked down across the beautiful valley of the Negrito river. To the left they could see right down to St Pierre and Santego Bay, with Cap Sarrat on the far side.

*Wyatt and Julie looked down across the beautiful valley
of the Negrito river.*

'It's so wonderful up in these mountains,' said Julie softly. 'I was hoping you would bring me up here again.'

'Is that why you came back to San Fernandez?' asked Wyatt quietly. He looked quickly at Julie, but she seemed very interested in the mountains. Wyatt decided to be brave. He put his arms around Julie, and said,

'How would you like to live up here? And marry me?'

Suddenly Julie's arms were around his neck. 'Oh Dave,' she cried, 'I'd like that very much.' Then for several minutes there was no conversation at all.

After a while Wyatt laughed and said, 'I didn't know what to think last night. You seemed much more interested in Causton and Hansen than in me!'

Julie smiled and pushed her hand through his hair. 'I was afraid, of course. I couldn't forget you, and so I had to come back to see you ... to find out. And your letters never told me anything!'

Wyatt laughed again. 'I was never very good at love letters. But now I won't have to write any,' he said happily.

They sat under a tree and talked for hours. They talked about their families, their hopes and plans, their new life together on San Fernandez. Wyatt had never felt so happy in his life. At last the shadows began to grow longer. Wyatt stood up and pulled Julie to her feet.

'Come on,' he said. 'Let's go and find a quiet dinner for two in St Pierre.'

They had not driven far along the road when Wyatt suddenly stopped the car again.

'What is it?' said Julie. 'What's the matter?'

Wyatt was staring at a house near the road. It was a small

wooden house, with no windows, and dried leaves for a roof. An old man was working busily round the house. There were several long ropes over the roof of the house, and the old man was fastening the ends of the ropes to strong sticks fixed in the ground.

'Just a minute, Julie,' said Wyatt. 'I'd like to talk to that man.'

He got out of the car and walked across to the house. The old man stopped his work and took the cigarette that Wyatt offered him. Wyatt lit it for him, and said,

'That's hard work. Why are you doing it?'

The old man looked surprised. 'I must make my house safe.' He put his nose to the cigarette. 'American – very good.'

Wyatt lit his own cigarette and turned to look at the house. 'The roof must not come off,' he agreed. 'And your family – are they here with you?'

'No. I have sent them north, over the mountains. When I have finished, I will go too.'

'You must be very afraid,' said Wyatt gently.

The old man looked at him. 'It is a time to be afraid. No man can fight the big wind.'

'The big wind,' repeated Wyatt quietly. 'How do you know that the wind is coming? And when will it come?'

The old man looked down the valley towards the sea. 'Two days,' he said. 'Perhaps three days. Not longer.'

Wyatt looked at the house again. 'When you go, leave the door open. The wind doesn't like closed doors.'

'Of course,' agreed the man. 'A closed door is unfriendly.' There was an amused look in his eyes. 'Perhaps there will be another wind soon, too. Worse than the hurricane. Favel is coming down from the mountains.'

'No man can fight the big wind,' said the old man.

Wyatt stared at him. 'But Favel is dead.'

The old man finished his cigarette. 'Perhaps,' he said.

Wyatt walked back to the car and got in. He looked at Julie. 'I'm sorry about the dinner,' he said, 'but I must get back to the Base at once.'

He started the engine, and as he drove, he told Julie what the old man had said. 'He knows the hurricane is coming. He doesn't know why, he doesn't know how, he just *knows*. And I think he's right. I can't explain it, but I think Mabel is going to hit San Fernandez. And Schelling is not going to believe it.'

He was driving very fast now, and Julie closed her eyes. 'It won't help if you kill us both in an accident.'

'Sorry.' Wyatt smiled and slowed down just a little.

—— 4 ——
Wyatt's warning

Wyatt left Julie at the hotel and drove on through the town and round to the Base. There were a lot of soldiers on the streets of St Pierre, but Wyatt thought only of Mabel. When he got inside the Base, he saw officers and sailors hurrying everywhere. Men with guns stood outside every building. Wyatt wondered what was happening.

He ran into his office and asked for the latest satellite pictures of Mabel. He sat down to study them carefully, and to check all the figures again and again. But it was no good. The information from the photographs and the figures said that Mabel would go past San Fernandez. It would come near enough to give the island only a few hours of strong winds and heavy rain. But Wyatt knew, and the old man in the mountains knew, that Mabel would hit the island.

Wyatt went to see Schelling, who told him he was crazy. They argued for some minutes, then Wyatt said he wanted to see Brooks, the Captain of the US Base.

'The Captain will be too busy to see you,' said Schelling angrily, but Wyatt refused to listen.

Half an hour later he was standing in front of Captain Brooks's desk.

'I understand from Schelling here,' said Brooks coolly, 'that you think this hurricane is going to hit the island. Please explain.'

'I agree with Schelling that it's a very small chance, sir,' said Wyatt carefully. 'But Mabel is a very bad piece of weather. And there is another danger, too. If Mabel does hit the island, she'll come from the south, straight into the shallow water of Santego Bay. The air pressure in the centre of Mabel is extraordinarily low; because of this, the sea under the centre will rise many metres above normal. In shallow water, this will be worse. The sea will rise by more than fifteen metres. The highest place on Cap Sarrat is, I believe, thirteen metres. There will be a huge tidal wave, which will go right over the top of the Base.'

He looked at Brooks, who said softly, 'Go on, Mr Wyatt.'

'In the hurricane in 1910 half the people in St Pierre died. Most of the town is no higher than Cap Sarrat. If Mabel hits, there will be 30,000 deaths in St Pierre. If the wind doesn't kill them first, the flood waters will kill them a few hours later.'

Captain Brooks looked at Schelling. 'I think we need another report on Mabel. Send a plane off at once.'

'Yes, sir.' Schelling turned and left the office.

Brooks then looked at Wyatt. 'I have a problem, Mr Wyatt,' he said calmly. 'Clearly, you think that I should get everybody out of Cap Sarrat because there is a chance, a small chance, that Mabel will hit us. And perhaps you are right. But Serrurier's army is getting ready to fight a war. There are rebels coming down from the mountains.' He gave a half-smile. 'The President of the United States will be very unhappy indeed if I leave this Base while there is a war on the island. So, I must stay, and hope that you are wrong about Mabel.'

Wyatt looked at him sadly. He could understand the problem. 'And the people of St Pierre? Can't you tell Serrurier to warn the people about the hurricane?'

'President Serrurier won't talk to me at all,' said Brooks, with another half-smile. 'He believes that the Americans have paid for the rebels' guns – which of course is not true. But you, Mr Wyatt, are not American. Perhaps he will listen to you.'

'I shouldn't think so,' said Wyatt, 'but I'll try.'

He left the Captain's office, and decided to go down to St Pierre immediately.

* * * * *

At the President's palace there were soldiers and police everywhere. There were several people waiting at the big front doors, and Wyatt saw John Causton among them. He went over to talk to him.

'You were right about Favel, then,' he said.

'Yes, I'm afraid so,' replied Causton. 'There's going to be some serious fighting soon. I'm waiting here for news. But what are you doing here?'

Quickly, Wyatt explained his fears about Mabel and his conversation with Captain Brooks. Causton listened carefully.

'And you think Serrurier will listen to you?' he asked.

'No,' said Wyatt, 'but I've got to try.'

'You're right,' said Causton. 'Come on. Let's talk our way in together. Two voices are louder than one.'

It took a long time. Wyatt and Causton argued first with one police officer, then with another. 'We have very important information for the President,' Causton said, again and again. At last they found themselves outside the door of the President's office. A soldier opened the door, and Wyatt and Causton walked down the long room to a small group of men at the far end. They were all army officers in uniform. Serrurier was in the middle – a small man, with angry eyes and a thin, hard voice.

'What is it? What is this important information?' He stared at them coldly.

Wyatt stepped forward. 'Mr President, in two days' time a dangerous hurricane will probably hit San Fernandez—'

'What!' shouted Serrurier. 'Have you come here to talk about the weather? I thought you had news of Favel! Favel, do you hear? I have to fight a battle tonight, and you talk to me about the weather!'

'Mr President, this hurricane—' began Causton.

'We do not have hurricanes in San Fernandez.' Serrurier stared at them with wild eyes.

'You had one in 1910,' said Wyatt quickly.

Serrurier's voice rose to a scream. 'We do not have hurricanes in San Fernandez. Get out! Officer, take these men out at once!'

Policemen ran in and pulled Wyatt and Causton down the

'What is this important information?' President Serrurier stared coldly at Wyatt and Causton.

long room. As the door closed, they could still hear Serrurier screaming, '*We do not have hurricanes in San Fernandez.*'

A few minutes later Wyatt and Causton were pushed violently out into the street.

'The man's crazy,' said Wyatt. 'Just crazy!'

'Well, we tried,' Causton said tiredly. 'What now?'

'I'm going to the hotel to get Julie, and then—'

Suddenly, Causton held his hand up. 'Listen! What's that noise? Is that your hurricane already?'

Wyatt listened. 'That's the sound of guns!' He looked at Causton. 'Favel has arrived!'

—— 5 ——
A night of fear

It was now late in the evening, but St Pierre was not asleep. The sound of guns was getting closer, and the people sat inside their houses behind locked doors. The street lighting had gone out, and Wyatt's car was stopped by the police or by soldiers on every street corner. He and Causton became tired of explaining who they were. At last they reached the hotel and hurried inside.

They found Julie in the bar with some other people. She ran at once into Wyatt's arms.

'Oh, Dave, are you all right? How did you get on?'

Wyatt told her everything that had happened. At the end, Julie said softly, 'Poor Dave. Nobody believes you about Mabel, do they?'

'Well, I do,' said Causton suddenly. Julie smiled at him warmly. Causton went on, 'I think Wyatt can smell bad weather coming. I'm a newsman, and I can smell trouble, but I often can't explain why.' He looked towards the other people at the bar. 'Who are they?' he asked.

'I know one of them,' said Wyatt. 'The old man, Mr Rawsthorne, is English. He's lived on the island for years.'

'The other two are American,' said Julie. 'Mrs Warmington is on holiday, and the man is Big Jim Dawson, the writer. You must know him. His books are very popular.' She turned to Wyatt. 'They all want to go to the US Base at Cap Sarrat. They think they'll be safe from the fighting there.'

'They won't be safe from Mabel,' said Wyatt. 'We must all get up into the mountains. Let's go and talk to them.'

They joined the three people at the bar, and began to discuss plans. The American woman was sure that the US Base was the safest place on the island. Patiently, Wyatt explained again about the hurricane. The Englishman, Rawsthorne, looked worried, and said,

'But it won't be easy to get out of St Pierre, you know. The rebels are coming down the Negrito valley, and I understand that there's fighting all round the town now.'

Suddenly, Jim Dawson looked out of the window into the street. 'Hey! Is that your car out there?' he said to Wyatt. 'Because there are six policemen trying to take it away, and we're going to need it!'

Wyatt jumped up and ran out through the hotel door. Dawson followed him. Julie began to follow, too, but Causton caught her arm. 'Take it easy,' he said. 'It's not a good idea to argue with the police tonight. They're frightened, and frightened men are dangerous.'

They stood in the shadows behind the door and watched through the window. They could see Dawson arguing loudly, and Wyatt trying to stop him. Then one of the policemen shouted, 'Spies! Spies! American spies!', and Wyatt and Dawson were marched away down the street, with guns at their backs.

Julie looked at Causton. Her face was white. 'They've arrested them! What will happen to them now?'

'I don't know,' said Causton, worried. 'I think I'll go after them. Perhaps I can help.' He turned to Julie. 'You stay here with the other two. Find a place to hide in the hotel. Don't go out! There'll be fighting in the streets soon. I'll be back as quickly as I can.'

Then he, too, disappeared into the dark street.

*   *   *   *   *

It was a long night. The sound of the guns grew louder and louder. After a few hours, the big guns stopped, and then there were new noises. The sounds of bombs exploding, of soldiers running through the streets, the screams and cries of dying men.

Julie, Rawsthorne, and Mrs Warmington hid in a small room upstairs, and listened to the battle. Julie stared into the darkness and thought about Wyatt. Where was he? What had happened to him? Once, they heard soldiers in the hotel bar, drinking and shouting and breaking furniture.

When morning came, Causton had still not returned. And neither had Wyatt or Dawson. By early afternoon Julie and

Wyatt and Dawson were marched away down the street, with guns at their backs.

Rawsthorne realized that they must leave the hotel and try to get up into the mountains. The frightened Mrs Warmington decided to go with them. They took food and blankets, and hurried out to Rawsthorne's car which was parked in a back street. They were not alone. Hundreds of other people were also trying to escape from the fighting in St Pierre.

───── 6 ─────
The battle for St Pierre

When Causton left the hotel, the group of policemen with Wyatt and Dawson had already disappeared. He decided to go to the big police station in the central square of the city, and hoped that he would find Wyatt and Dawson there.

But it was not that easy. He had to go all through the narrow back streets, hide while soldiers passed, then move carefully on again, then hide again. When at last he came near the square, he saw that he was too late. There was already a fierce battle going on, all around the square. Bullets were flying through the air, and several buildings were already on fire. As he watched, he saw a bomb explode and smoke filled the street.

'These are Favel's soldiers,' thought Causton. 'He's reached the centre already! By tomorrow his men will control the town. But does he know about Wyatt's hurricane, I wonder?'

Another bomb exploded not far away. Causton turned and ran back into the narrow streets, away from the city centre. He found an empty shop, climbed in through a broken window, and hid in the back. He was a reporter, and had been in battles before. He knew that it would not be safe to come out for several hours.

When he did come out, it was early morning. He returned to the central square. The fighting had moved away, but he could still hear the guns. At the corner of the square he saw an army car with a tall, fair-haired man next to it. The man was wearing the green uniform of Favel's army. Causton ran up to him.

'I need to see Julio Favel,' he said quickly. 'Do you know where he is?'

The man stared at him. 'Yes, I do. I'm Manning, his second officer. And who are you?'

'Causton. I'm a reporter. I've got some important news for Favel.'

Manning looked Causton up and down. 'OK,' he said. 'Get in.' They both got into the car and Manning started the engine. 'What's this news about?' he asked.

'There's a man called Wyatt ...' began Causton.

*   *   *   *   *

Wyatt and Dawson listened to the battle for St Pierre from a prison. The police had locked them up in a small stone building behind the central police station. This probably saved their lives because, at about four o'clock in the morning, several bombs hit the police station and most of the building was destroyed.

The noise was terrible. Broken glass fell into the room and the walls shook. Wyatt and Dawson lay on the floor, with their arms over their heads. Then more bombs exploded all round the square outside, and they heard men screaming and shouting. The noise seemed to go on for hours, but at last it became quieter. The battle had moved on.

'Well!' said Dawson. 'We're still alive, I suppose.'

He tried to laugh bravely, but there was a shake in his voice. He had been very frightened indeed during the battle. He – Big Jim Dawson, who was not afraid of anything, and who wrote famous books about wars and fighting ... and big strong men like himself.

'It's funny, you know,' he went on. 'I write about this kind of adventure in my books, but I've never been in one before.'

'This isn't an adventure story,' said Wyatt coldly. 'It's real life, and a real war. And we've got to get out of here. I must find Julie and make sure she's safe.'

'Yeah, you're right.' Dawson looked at the young man who was now walking round and round their small prison. When the police had arrested them, Wyatt had told him to keep quiet and not argue. But Dawson had not listened, and so the angry police had locked them both up. And while Wyatt was worrying about his girl, he, Dawson, was only worrying about himself. He began to feel ashamed.

'I guess I should say sorry, Wyatt. Next time I start to make trouble for you, you can hit me over the head first.'

Wyatt smiled. 'Perhaps I will. But never mind that now. Let's get out of here.'

He was now standing next to the wall, feeling it with his hands. 'I think one of those bombs has damaged this wall. Perhaps we can push some stones out and make a hole big enough to climb through. Let's try it!'

They broke a chair into pieces and then used the bits of wood to dig at the wall. It was hard work and took a long time, but

They used the bits of wood to dig at the wall.

after several hours they had a hole just big enough for a man's body. Carefully, they crawled through the hole and found themselves in a narrow side street a few metres from the central square of the city. There was nobody in the street, so they went quickly down to the corner and looked out.

The square was full of dead bodies. They lay everywhere, quiet and still in the bright evening sunlight. Sick and shaken, Wyatt and Dawson turned away, and began to cross the city towards the hotel.

When they finally got there, it was late evening. There was nobody in the hotel, but they could see that the soldiers had been there. Broken bottles and glasses lay everywhere in the bar. They searched all the rooms, and it was Dawson who found the message from Julie. It was a piece of paper fixed to a cupboard door under the stairs. Wyatt read it quickly.

'She left with the others at two o'clock this afternoon,' he said. 'They went east, up into the mountains. I hope they haven't run into another battle.' He sounded very tired.

Dawson looked at him. 'Let's find some food and get a few hours sleep before we go after them.'

Wyatt stared at the note in his hand. 'There's something I must do before we leave St Pierre,' he said. 'I must find Favel and warn him about the hurricane.'

*   *   *   *   *

They were woken at three o'clock in the morning. Soldiers were searching the hotel. Wyatt and Dawson looked down the stairs and saw a tall, fair-haired man giving orders. He looked up and saw them.

'I'm looking for a man called Wyatt,' he called.

Wyatt stepped forward. 'That's me,' he said. 'Who—'

'Favel wants to see you. Come on, I'm in a hurry. I'll explain while we drive.'

Still half-asleep, Wyatt and Dawson followed him to his car. As they drove, the fair-haired man talked.

'I'm Manning, Favel's number two. An English newsman came in yesterday with some story about a hurricane. He says you're the man who knows all about it. I've been looking for you all over the city.'

＊   ＊   ＊   ＊   ＊

Favel was using the post office building for his war office. His soldiers had now taken most of St Pierre and had driven Serrurier's army out to the north and south-east. There was still fierce fighting on the edges of the city, and smoke from burning buildings rose high into the night sky.

When they arrived, Manning took them straight into a big room at the back of the building and left them there. Causton was standing by a window and hurried over to them.

'Welcome back,' he said. 'You managed to get out of prison, then.'

Wyatt smiled. 'Only because we were bombed. What happened to you? And is Favel winning this war?'

'I'll tell you later,' said Causton. 'Favel wants to talk to you now. I've told him about Mabel, but I don't think he believes me.'

At that moment Favel entered the room, followed by Manning and several other officers. Favel was a thin, but strong-looking man, with an intelligent face and very blue eyes. He turned to Wyatt at once.

'Ah, Mr Wyatt,' he said politely. 'I want to hear all about this hurricane of yours.'

Wyatt knew that this was his last chance. Favel *must* believe him. Wyatt began to talk. He told Favel the facts and figures, carefully and honestly. He told him about the old man in the hills, and about his own strong feeling that Mabel would change direction and hit the island.

'But you haven't had any new information for nearly two days,' Manning said. 'And why hasn't Brooks left the Base?'

'I can understand that,' said Favel calmly. 'Brooks is afraid we'll take the Base if he leaves, and that the Americans will never get it back. Please continue, Mr Wyatt.'

Wyatt explained the danger of floods. 'There could be a tidal wave from the sea as high as 15 metres,' he said.

Favel's eyes suddenly narrowed. 'Show me,' he ordered. He opened a large map out on the table.

'Nowhere below the 25-metre contour line will be safe,' Wyatt said. With a black pen he drew a big circle round St Pierre. 'There will be serious floods in the city, on Cap Sarrat, and on all the low ground round Santego Bay. And also up the Negrito valley, of course.'

'*If* you are right about this hurricane,' said Manning.

'I *am* right,' Wyatt said strongly. 'Mabel will hit San Fernandez sometime tonight or tomorrow.'

Favel stared at the map. Then he looked up at Wyatt.

'I believe you, Mr Wyatt,' he said quietly. 'And from now on, you will be my one-man weather information office.' He turned to Manning. 'This hurricane is now a fact. So, we must change our plans.'

Manning gave Wyatt a very angry look. 'But Julio, we're fighting a war! You can't—'

'I must,' said Favel. 'These are my people, Charles. There are sixty thousand of them in this city. I can't take a chance with their lives. Now go away, and let me think.'

——— 7 ———
Favel's plan

Two hours passed. Wyatt was up on the roof of the post office building with Dawson and Causton. It was a tall building, and they could see right across Santego Bay to Cap Sarrat. The sky began to grow lighter in the east. There were no clouds, and no wind, but it was very hot. Manning came up on to the roof to see Wyatt.

'Any news?' he asked. Wyatt shook his head.

Suddenly, Causton said, 'What's happening at the US Base? Look!'

They looked, and saw plane after plane taking off from Cap Sarrat. They saw first one ship, then another and another, begin to move out to sea. The US Navy was on the move.

'Brooks is leaving the Base,' Wyatt said excitedly. 'They'll have the latest satellite pictures of Mabel. They must know that she's changed direction!'

'My God!' shouted Manning. 'There *is* going to be a hurricane.'

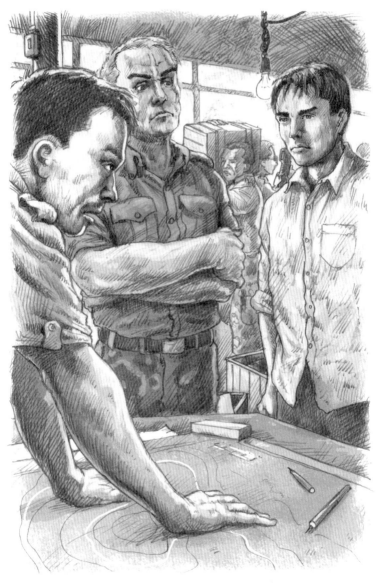

'So, the big wind is coming,' said Favel. 'What should we do, Mr Wyatt?

The room downstairs was full of people. 'So, the big wind is coming,' said Favel. 'What should we do, Mr Wyatt?'

'Get everybody out of the city,' Wyatt said at once. 'Perhaps Serrurier will agree to stop fighting while—'

The soldiers laughed. 'Serrurier?' said Favel. 'He doesn't care about the people. And he knows that we don't have hurricanes here. He told you – remember? No, we must continue fighting and hold back his army, while we get the people out.' He turned to Manning. 'Charles, this is your job. I want you to get everybody out of the city, except the army. Send the people up the Negrito valley, but keep them well away from the river. You can have two thousand soldiers to help you.'

'Julio!' said Manning. He held his head between his hands. 'We can't do it! We haven't enough—'

'If the people won't move,' continued Favel, 'push them. If necessary, you'll have to shoot a few. There's no time to explain or to argue with them. Just get them out. In ten hours from now I want every man, woman, and child out of St Pierre.'

'Impossible!' said Manning.

Favel looked at him. 'Do it, Charles,' he said softly.

Manning closed his eyes. 'OK,' he said. 'We get them out. Then what?'

'Then we'll let Serrurier and his army take St Pierre. For the first time ever, a hurricane will become a weapon of war.' Favel smiled, gently.

The room was silent for a second. Then Wyatt found his voice. 'You can't do that!' he said shakily.

'Can't I?' Favel turned his fierce blue eyes on Wyatt. 'I've been trying to kill those men with bullets and with bombs. And they want to kill me and my men. Why shouldn't I let the hurricane have them? Many of my men will die while we fight to give the people time to get out.'

'I warned you about the hurricane in order to save lives,' said Wyatt, 'not to take them.'

'Think, man!' said Favel angrily. 'What do you want me to do? Leave *my* men in the city to drown in the floods? I must take my men out, and when we leave the city, of course Serrurier's army will come in. I'm not *asking* them to come in.'

'How far out of the city will you go?' asked Wyatt.

'We will stop on the hills around the city, at the 25-metre contour line. You told us that we'll be just above the floods there.'

'If you go higher, then Serrurier's soldiers can follow you to higher ground, where they'll be safe.' Wyatt was almost shouting now.

'No!' Favel banged his hand down on the table. 'I don't wish to fight any more battles. Let the hurricane do its work.'

'But it's murder!' Wyatt said wildly.

Favel stared at him. 'War *is* murder,' he said.

*　　*　　*　　*　　*

Wyatt spent most of the morning on the roof, staring miserably at the clear blue sky. He wanted desperately to go and look for Julie. Where was she? Would she find a safe place to shelter during the hurricane? He tried not to think about Favel's terrible plan.

At one o'clock Causton came up to see him. 'Anything happening?' he asked.

'Mabel's on her way,' said Wyatt. 'Look at those clouds.'

A few thin, high clouds were appearing in the south. The air was hot and heavy. There was no wind at all.

Causton looked at Wyatt's unhappy face. 'You're still angry with Favel, aren't you?'

'He's as bad as Serrurier.'

'Look, Wyatt,' Causton said, 'you're not thinking clearly. It's not an easy plan, you know. Favel has five thousand men against Serrurier's fifteen thousand. He was lucky to take St Pierre at all, and he hasn't won the war yet. Serrurier's army is already beginning to attack, from the west and the south-east. Favel has only three thousand men to fight, while the other two thousand get the people out of the city. And then Favel has to get his men out, and up to the 25-metre line – if Serrurier's guns haven't killed them first.'

Both men were silent for a while. Then Wyatt asked, 'Have they finished moving the people out?'

'No. It's difficult to move sixty thousand people in a few hours.' Causton said no more. He had been out in the city all morning. Favel's soldiers were pulling people from their homes, and driving them like sheep along the streets. There was no time to explain, to be patient. People who tried to turn back fell under the feet of the crowds. People who argued were shot. Dead bodies lay at every street corner. It was terrible, cruel, violent. But it was necessary.

At three o'clock heavy, grey clouds began to move across the sky. It was hotter than ever, and there was a thin circle of cloud around the sun. Wyatt went down to see Favel.

'Mabel will hit at about five o'clock,' he told Favel. 'You'll have winds of about a hundred kilometres an hour, and they'll get worse very quickly. The tidal wave will hit probably soon after six o'clock. And in the next twenty-four hours you'll have between twelve and twenty-five centimetres of rain.'

Favel turned to Manning. 'We'll have to hurry, Charles. Start moving our men out now.'

'Serrurier is pushing hard from the south,' said Manning tiredly. 'I'll do my best, Julio.' He left the room quickly.

Favel turned back to Wyatt. 'Thank you, Mr Wyatt,' he said calmly. 'Please inform me at once of any change.'

The sound of guns was now much louder, as Serrurier's army fought its way back into the city. Slowly, Favel's soldiers moved backwards street by street, while the last of the people were pushed out of the city. Many soldiers died. At four o'clock Favel ordered his men to blow up the big guns. There was no time to move them. Twenty minutes later Favel gave the order to leave the city. From the back of Favel's army car, Wyatt looked back through the window to the south. Low, grey clouds now covered the sky, and the smoke from burning buildings was driven sideways by the rising wind.

It was half past four in the afternoon.

—— 8 ——
Mabel hits the island

Julie sat with her back against a banana tree and stared up at the sky. The sun had disappeared behind thick grey cloud, and a cool wind was beginning to blow. It was half past four in the afternoon.

She turned to the man next to her. 'I think we should move

*The smoke from burning buildings was driven sideways
by the rising wind.*

on now,' she said. 'The weather's getting worse.'

Rawsthorne opened his eyes. His face was tired and grey. 'Yes, my dear, you're right. We must find a safer place than this field. We'll go north, across this valley in front of us and up over the next hill.'

They woke Mrs Warmington, and the three of them moved forward through the field of banana trees.

The last two days had not been easy. It had been impossible to drive out of St Pierre because there were so many people on the roads. So they had left the car and walked. As evening came, the road became crowded with Serrurier's soldiers, who were running from the battle of St Pierre. Julie and the others left the road and spent the night in a field.

In the morning there were still a lot of soldiers around, so they kept away from the road. Rawsthorne knew the island well and he decided that they should turn north. 'We must get away from Serrurier's army,' he had said. 'We'll go north over the hills towards the Negrito valley.'

It was difficult, rocky ground, and they could not walk fast. Rawsthorne was an old man and his heart was not strong. Mrs Warmington was fat and lazy, and wore fashionable shoes that hurt her feet. She was not an intelligent woman and she argued all the time in a thin, high voice. Julie was very tired of her.

By half past five the wind had become very strong. It beat fiercely at their backs as they climbed the last few metres to the top of the hill. Quickly, they climbed down the other side to get out of the wind and then stopped to rest for a minute. They were now at the top of the Negrito valley and could see down to the river three hundred metres below.

Rawsthorne stared. 'My God,' he said. 'What's happening down there?'

Hundreds, thousands of people were moving slowly along the valley.

'They must be from St Pierre,' said Rawsthorne. 'But why have they come up here? I wonder ...' He did not finish, but Julie understood.

'There's only one reason,' she said, and her voice shook with happiness. 'It's Dave. It must be. He's managed to warn the people of St Pierre about the hurricane. He's alive!'

Rawsthorne put his hand on her arm. 'I hope so,' he said kindly. 'But I think we must find somewhere to shelter from the storm now.'

A few minutes later they found some large rocks and underneath them, in the side of the hill, was a large hole, almost a cave. It was just big enough for three people, and as they crawled into it, the first heavy drops of rain began to fall.

*   *   *   *   *

As Favel's car drove up the road to the hills, the sound of Serrurier's guns was not far behind. His soldiers were moving in fast to take the city back from the rebels.

Wyatt tried one last time. 'Must there be more killing?' he asked Favel.

'It's too late,' said Favel. 'My men will be lucky if they can get out of the city in time. I can do nothing more.' The blue eyes looked at Wyatt. 'You must talk to your God, Mr Wyatt, and I must talk to mine,' he said gently.

At the 25-metre contour line, Favel's men had been busy. On

Hundreds, thousands of people were moving slowly along the valley.

the northern side of a long, low ridge they were digging deep holes everywhere. They would shelter in these holes from the storm. At the top of the ridge other soldiers lay with their guns and looked down the hill towards the city.

Dawson was waiting for Wyatt near the top of the ridge. 'Hi,' he said. 'Causton's chosen a nice, comfortable hole for us. Just right for the three of us.'

They stood together and looked down the hill towards the city, and beyond it to the sea. The southern sky was now filled with black, mountainous clouds, and the wind was becoming stronger every minute. As they watched, groups of Favel's soldiers appeared on the edge of the city and began to run up the hill towards the ridge.

'That's the last of Favel's men now,' said Causton behind them. He had to shout above the noise of the wind. 'I hope Serrurier's soldiers don't try to attack us up here.'

'This war will be over in ten minutes,' said Wyatt. 'No one can fight a war in a hurricane.'

*   *   *   *   *

More than five centimetres of rain fell in the first hour – huge, heavy drops as big as stones. They hit the body like bullets. Wyatt kept his head down and sat with Causton and Dawson in a hole full of water. All around them rainwater ran in rivers down the ridge, turning the soft ground to mud everywhere. Above their heads, the wind was wild and violent. It was already blowing, Wyatt thought, at about 120 kilometres an hour.

Causton was frightened. He had not realized that the storm would be so bad. He put his mouth next to Wyatt's ear, and shouted, 'How long will this go on?' He could only just hear Wyatt's answering shout.

'About eight hours. Then it'll stop for a short time. Then we'll have about another ten hours.'

'Will it get worse?'

'It hasn't really started yet.'

Causton thought Wyatt sounded amused. He pushed himself deeper into the mud and covered his ears with his hands.

Night came, and the savage wind grew more and more violent. Lightning flashed across the blackness of the sky. Hour after hour, the hurricane screamed like an animal in pain. Soon after midnight the wind reached speeds of more than 250 kilometres an hour. The noise alone was frightening – an endless, savage howl. It was impossible to move, to speak, to think, in that terrible wind.

Once, when Dawson opened his eyes, he saw a tree flying past above their heads. He felt the ground shake as the tree crashed down not far beyond their hole.

Hours passed. Then at last Wyatt noticed a change. The rain had stopped now, and he thought the wind was less violent. He cleaned the mud off his watch. Four o'clock. Very carefully, he pushed his hand up out of the hole. Yes, he was right. The wind was not so strong. What had happened out there? He had to know.

Slowly, he pulled himself out of the hole and began to crawl upwards on his stomach through the mud. The wind tore at his wet clothes and he was afraid to lift his head too high. At last he reached the top of the ridge and carefully lifted his face from the mud.

He stared into the darkness down the hill. At first he could

Hour after hour, the hurricane screamed like an animal in pain.

see nothing, but he thought he could hear the sound of water. He stared again. A flash of lightning lit up the sky, and then Wyatt saw a very frightening thing.

Not more than two hundred metres away was the sea – a stormy grey sea with angry little waves. The wind blew fiercely into Wyatt's face and he could taste salt water on his lips.

St Pierre had disappeared, drowned under the sea.

——— 9 ———
The eye of the hurricane

As the first grey light of morning touched the sky, people began to move out of their holes. Wyatt and Dawson stood on top of the ridge and looked down over the city. The flood waters had already dropped a little, and they could see that only a few buildings were still standing. They saw no soldiers. There was no movement at all from the broken city.

Dawson turned away. 'My ears ache terribly,' he said.

'It's because of the low pressure in the eye of the hurricane,' Wyatt explained. He looked up at the thick grey cloud. The air was still and heavy. 'Another hour or two, and the wind will be back. Let's go and find Favel.'

They walked with Causton along the muddy road towards Favel's headquarters. Suddenly Causton stopped and stared.

'My God,' he said in horror. 'Look at that.'

Not far away was the dead body of a man, half-in and half-out of a hole. His head lay sideways in a very unnatural way. The wind had broken his neck.

Wyatt walked on. He knew that there would be many accidental deaths in this hurricane. But he could not stop thinking about another death, the death of an army of men – also killed in the hurricane, but not accidentally.

Favel's headquarters was a number of holes in the ground. Officers were hurrying up with reports, and soon Favel called Wyatt to him.

'Your hurricane was as bad as you promised, Mr Wyatt,' he said. 'I'm sending some of my men up the Negrito valley to help the people. How long have we got before the wind returns?'

For some minutes they looked at maps and discussed the floods and the storm damage to roads and bridges. Wyatt told him as much as he could about the second half of the hurricane.

'I'm very grateful for your help, Mr Wyatt,' Favel said gently.

Wyatt walked back to join Dawson, who was talking to Manning. Dawson turned quickly to Wyatt and said excitedly, 'Hey, Manning tells me he's had a report about some foreigners up the Negrito valley. About eight kilometres up. Perhaps it's your Julie and the others.'

Wyatt's heart gave a violent jump inside him. 'I'm going up there at once,' he said wildly, and turned to leave.

Manning caught his arm. 'You'll never get there on foot before the storm starts again. Look, you can borrow my army car. I kept it safe from the hurricane.'

*   *   *   *   *

Wyatt drove as fast as he could along the muddy roads. Dawson sat beside him. He had now lived through a battle and the first half of a hurricane, and was no longer a frightened man. He felt he had learnt more about danger and fear than he had ever known before. Perhaps his next book would be better because of that. He felt grateful towards Wyatt – this honest, brave, stubborn young man, who seemed to have no fear for himself at all. Dawson wanted to help him in this crazy search for his girl.

'I don't understand Manning,' Wyatt said suddenly. 'He's English, isn't he? Why is he fighting for Favel and San Fernandez?'

'He's a soldier who goes where the work is,' replied Dawson.

'Oh, I see. He does it for the money.'

'It's not only for the money,' said Dawson. 'He chooses which side he fights for, you know. He believes that Favel will be a much better president for the people of San Fernandez than Serrurier was. He's an interesting man. I had a long talk with him back in St Pierre.' He smiled. 'Perhaps I'll put him in my next book.'

'Don't put me in any of your books,' warned Wyatt.

Dawson laughed. 'Why not? You'll be a famous man because of your hurricane.'

After four kilometres they had to leave the car. Floods had washed the road away, and it had disappeared down the hillside in a sea of mud. They began to hurry east along the top of the valley. Down below them the flooded Negrito river lay like a small sea. Everywhere, the ground was covered with fallen trees and broken branches. Trees that were still standing had lost all their leaves. Dawson looked over to the south and saw that the sky was already growing dark again. Lightning flashed through the great black clouds.

'Mabel will be with us soon,' he said.

Wyatt stared desperately up the valley. 'Yes. We'll have to

Below them the flooded Negrito river lay like a small sea.

stop. We'll move down lower and find a place to dig in.'

Dawson looked at Wyatt's worried face. 'Julie's a sensible girl. She'll be all right.'

'I hope so,' Wyatt said unhappily.

Quickly, they dug a shallow hole in the stony ground and lay down in it. The wind rose to a thin, high scream.

*   *   *   *   *

Julie and the others had lived through the first half of the hurricane, but it had been a bad night. Their little cave under the rocks was safe from the wind, but not from the water. The rainwater had run in rivers down the hillside and over the rocks above them. It fell in a wall of dirty brown water on their legs as they lay in the cave. Then the wind grew stronger and began to blow the water into the cave. Several times they were nearly drowned in a sudden flood.

The night passed, and daylight brought the calm eye of the hurricane. The three of them crawled thankfully out of the cave and sat on a low rock.

Down below, the bottom of the valley was covered with a great sheet of water. The Negrito river had flooded, and destroyed roads and bridges and farms. They could see people moving about above the floods.

Rawsthorne looked up at the grey sky. 'The wind will be back soon, I think. Didn't Wyatt tell us that, my dear?' he said, turning to Julie.

'I think so,' she said. 'After about an hour.' Her body was tired and aching, but her clothes were already drying in the hot, still air.

'Don't be stupid,' said Mrs Warmington crossly. 'The storm

has finished. There's no wind at all now.' She stood up and pulled her skirt straight. 'I'm going down into the valley. I'll find someone there who'll take me to the US Navy Base.' She began to walk down the hill.

'You'll be safer up here in our cave,' Julie called after her, but Mrs Warmington did not listen. Julie turned to Rawsthorne, and immediately forgot about Mrs Warmington. Rawsthorne's eyes were closed and his lips were grey.

'Mr Rawsthorne, are you all right?' Julie asked in a worried voice.

Rawsthorne opened his eyes. 'Hurricanes aren't good for an old heart like mine. But don't worry, my dear.' He smiled tiredly, and closed his eyes again.

Julie stayed by his side. He was clearly too ill to walk down the hill, and there was no time to get help. And where would she get help from?

Soon the wind began to drive fiercely up the valley. It sang wildly in the leafless branches of the tall tree just behind their rock.

'I think it's time to get back into our cave,' Julie said gently.

She helped the old man to his feet. The wind gave a sudden howl above their heads and there was a terrible tearing sound from the tree. Julie looked up, and saw the tree beginning to fall towards them.

'Look out!' she screamed.

But they could not move quickly enough on the muddy ground. The tree crashed down on top of them, and the world went black.

—— 10 ——
Peace at last

*F*or ten more hours the hurricane howled and screamed and crashed over San Fernandez. It tore plants and trees out of the ground, it destroyed buildings, it brought death to many of the thousands of people in the Negrito valley. But at last the big wind itself began to die.

By three o'clock in the afternoon it was just possible for a man to stand up in the wind. Favel's tired soldiers climbed out of their holes and caves and began to move up the Negrito valley. They tried to help the people, but thousands were hurt or sick. Doctors, medicine, food, blankets – all these things were needed desperately.

On Cap Sarrat Base the flood waters had gone down, but most of the buildings were badly damaged. Causton stood on the airfield at the Base, near Favel and a group of his officers, and watched as the US Navy helicopters landed. The green and gold flag of San Fernandez now flew from the top of one of the buildings. Causton smiled. Favel did not want to take the Base back from the Americans, but he wanted them to pay more money for it.

The first helicopter landed, and Causton watched as Captain Brooks got out. Favel moved forward. 'Welcome back to Cap Sarrat,' he said. 'I am Julio Favel.'

'Brooks. United States Navy.' The two men shook hands. Captain Brooks did not look at the green and gold flag.

'What do you need most, Mr Favel, and where do you need it? The five helicopters behind me are full of doctors.'

'Welcome back to Cap Sarrat,' said Favel.

'We need everything, but most help is needed in the Negrito valley.'

'The Negrito?' Brooks looked surprised. 'Then you got your people out of St Pierre?'

'With the help of your Mr Wyatt. That is a very brave and honest young man.'

They began to walk up the airfield. 'Yes,' said Brooks. 'I wish I had ...'

*   *   *   *   *

Dawson followed Wyatt along the side of the valley. He was tired and hungry, and covered in mud. But he knew that Wyatt was desperate with worry about Julie. Together, they searched up and down the hillside, through the crowds of people, who sat or lay on the muddy, broken ground.

The people were slowly realizing that the terrible storm had finished. Some had begun to move, and were helping Favel's men with the rescue work. But others still sat on the ground and stared in front of them at nothing. Dawson saw one woman holding a dead child in her arms. She did not seem to realize that the child was dead.

'We can't do anything to help her,' Wyatt said sadly. They moved on to continue their search. Dawson saw another group of Favel's men higher up the hill and went to ask them for news of any foreigners. Twenty minutes later he came running up behind Wyatt.

'I've seen that American woman, Mrs Warmington,' he said quickly. 'She says that she left Julie and Rawsthorne higher up, just below the top of the hill. There's a cave under some rocks.'

They climbed as fast as they could up the hillside. Behind them the American helicopters were beginning to land at the bottom of the valley.

Another hour passed before they found Julie and Rawsthorne. Dawson saw them first. He and Wyatt pulled and pushed at the tree and managed to lift it off the two still bodies. Poor Rawsthorne was dead, but Julie was still alive. Her legs were

Julie was still alive.

broken and her face was white with pain, but she opened her eyes
and smiled as Wyatt put his arms around her.

Dawson went to fetch help, and Wyatt sat gratefully in the
mud, holding Julie's hands.

                    *   *   *   *   *

And so Wyatt went back to Cap Sarrat Base. He did not know
that in a day or two his name would be in all the world's
newspapers. He would be a famous man, the man who had saved
a city's people – and the man who had destroyed an army.

He knew nothing of all this. He felt tired and miserable. He
felt that he had failed as a weatherman, as a scientist, because
too many people had died in his hurricane.

David Wyatt was still very young. He was an honest,
intelligent, and hard-working scientist, but he did not understand
the ways of the world.

GLOSSARY

attack (*v*)   to start fighting violently

base   a place where part of an army, navy, etc. live and keep their weapons

bay (*n*)   an area of sea with land around it on three sides

believe   to think that something is true or right

blow (past tense **blew**)   when air moves, a wind is blowing

cave   a hole in the side of a hill or under the ground

city   a big, important town

control (*v*)   to have power over something; to be the person who gives orders

contour line   a line on a map which shows how high the ground is above sea level

crawl   to move slowly on your stomach, using your hands and knees to push

cruel   not kind; bringing pain or trouble to others

desperate   having no hope and ready to do any wild or dangerous thing

direction   where something or someone is going

draw (past tense **drew**)   to make pictures or lines with a pen, pencil, etc.

drown   to die in water because you cannot breathe

fierce   violent and angry, very strong

flash (*n*)   a sudden very bright light, that comes and goes quickly

flood (*n*)   a lot of water from rain or the sea, which covers the land

God (**my God**)   the one great being who made the world; an expression of great surprise or horror

headquarters   the place from where an army, a company, etc. is controlled

helicopter   a kind of aeroplane with big, turning blades on top

horror   a feeling of very great fear or dislike

howl (*n*)   the long, loud cry made by a dog or wild animal

huge   very, very big

hurricane   a dangerous storm with very strong, violent winds

instrument   any kind of machine or tool for measuring or
    collecting information

lightning   a sudden bright light in the sky during a storm

mountainous   looking like a mountain

mud   very soft, wet earth

navy   all the warships of a country, with officers and men

normal   usual, ordinary

pressure   the force or weight of something, e.g. of the air in the
    atmosphere

rebel (*n*)   someone who fights against the government of his
    country

rescue (*n*)   saving or bringing someone away from danger

ridge   a long, narrow piece of high land on the top of hills

rise (past tense **rose**)   to go upwards

rope   very thick, strong string

satellite   a spacecraft that goes around the earth and sends back
    radio and television signals, etc., to earth

savage   wild, very fierce

scientist   somebody who studies or works with science (the
    study of natural things)

shelter (*v*)   to find somewhere safe from bad weather or danger

sideways   to one side

speed   how quickly something moves

stare (*v*)   to look at someone or something very hard for a long
    time

stubborn   not wanting to change; very determined

tear (past tense **tore**)   to pull something to pieces very roughly

tidal wave one huge wave from the sea, caused by a storm or
  earthquake
war fighting between countries or between people in one
  country
warn to tell someone about danger that is coming
wave (*n*) a moving 'hill' of water in the sea
weapon something to fight with, e.g. a gun, bomb, knife

ACTIVITIES

Before Reading

1 **Read the story introduction on the first page of the book, and the back cover. What do you think is going to happen in this story? Choose Y (Yes) or N (No) for each of these ideas.**

  1 If the hurricane hits San Fernandez . . .

    a) thousands of people will die. Y/N

    b) it will destroy many buildings. Y/N

    c) it will stop the war. Y/N

  2 If the hurricane does not hit San Fernandez . . .

    a) David Wyatt will be angry. Y/N

    b) David Wyatt will lose his job. Y/N

    c) the war will happen and thousands of people will still die. Y/N

  3 If there is a war, it will be between . . .

    a) San Fernandez and the USA. Y/N

    b) San Fernandez and Britain. Y/N

    c) two groups of people on San Fernandez. Y/N

    d) San Fernandez and another Caribbean island. Y/N

2 What is the best thing for people to do if hurricane Mabel does hit San Fernandez? Look at these ideas and decide which are sensible, and which are not sensible. Explain why you think this.

People will be safe in the hurricane if they . . .

1 stay at home in St Pierre and shut the doors and windows.
2 go out into a field and shelter under some big trees.
3 dig a hole in the ground and hide in it.
4 drive to high ground away from the sea and stay in their car.
5 go up into the mountains and hide in a cave.
6 go to the top of the tallest building in St Pierre.
7 leave the country by plane before the hurricane arrives.
8 go out to sea in a boat.

3 The title of Chapter 1 is *Flying into the hurricane*. Can you guess the answers to these questions?

1 Who flies into the hurricane?
2 Why do they do this?
3 Will the plane crash into the sea?
4 If they get back safely, what will they do afterwards?

ACTIVITIES

While Reading

Read Chapters 1, 2, and 3, and then rewrite these sentences with the correct information.

1 Wyatt didn't know very much about hurricanes.
2 In the 'eye' of the hurricane the winds were very violent.
3 Schelling thought that Mabel could hit San Fernandez.
4 Laura was one of Wyatt's girlfriends.
5 Julio Favel was a friend of President Serrurier.
6 Julie wasn't interested in Wyatt.
7 The old man was making his house safe because he knew Favel was coming down from the mountains.

Before you read Chapter 4 (the title is *Wyatt's warning*), can you guess which of these people will believe his warning?

1 Schelling.
2 The Captain of the US Navy Base.
3 John Causton, the newspaper reporter.
4 President Serrurier.
5 Julie Marlowe.

Read Chapters 5, 6, and 7. Who said this, and to whom? What, or who, were they talking about?

1 'They're frightened, and frightened men are dangerous.'
2 'I guess I should say sorry.'

3 'There's something I must do before we leave St Pierre.'
4 'I can't take a chance with their lives.'
5 'They'll have the latest satellite pictures of Mabel.'
6 'Impossible!'
7 'I'm not *asking* them to come in.'
8 'But it's murder!'

Read Chapters 8 and 9, then answer these questions.

1 At half past four in the afternoon, where was Wyatt, and where was Julie, and who were they with?
2 Why did Julie believe that Wyatt was still alive?
3 Where was Favel's army when the hurricane began?
4 What speeds did the wind reach during the worst part of the hurricane?
5 What frightening thing did Wyatt see from the ridge?
6 Why did Wyatt and Dawson hurry off to the Negrito valley during the eye of the hurricane?
7 How did Dawson feel about the hurricane?
8 Where were Julie and Rawsthorne during the second half of the hurricane?

Before you read Chapter 10 (the title is *Peace at last*), can you guess how the story ends?

1 Will Wyatt find Julie, and will she be alive or dead?
2 Will Favel take the US Base on Cap Sarrat and refuse to allow the Americans to come back?
3 What will the Americans do?

ACTIVITIES

After Reading

1 **Put this summary about Chapters 5 and 6 into the right order, which will make a paragraph of five sentences.**

   1 to follow them to the police station and try to help.
   2 At Favel's headquarters Causton told Favel about Wyatt's hurricane,
   3 there was already a fierce battle going on,
   4 When Wyatt and Dawson ran out to the car outside the hotel,
   5 In the morning he returned to the square and met Manning,
   6 Immediately afterwards, Causton left the hotel
   7 and Favel then sent his men to search for Wyatt all over the city.
   8 they were arrested by the police and taken away.
   9 so he spent the night hiding in an empty shop.
   10 But by the time he reached the central city square,
   11 who agreed to take him at once to see Favel.

2 **Now rewrite the rest of the summary. Change the words in italic to pronouns (e.g. *they, it, this*) or leave them out, and use these linking words to make five longer sentences.**

   which / because / when / but / so / and

   Favel's men found Wyatt in the hotel. *Favel's men* took *Wyatt* to Favel's headquarters. Favel listened carefully to what Wyatt said about the hurricane. *Favel* decided to believe *Wyatt*. *Favel* did not want to take a chance with his people's lives. Two hours later the US Navy left the Base on Cap Sarrat. Everybody realized that the hurricane was now certain. Favel then made a plan. *Favel's plan* would use the hurricane as a weapon of war. Wyatt was very unhappy about *Favel's plan*. *Wyatt* couldn't do anything about *Favel's plan*.

3 **Before Wyatt sees Captain Brooks in Chapter 4, the Captain has a talk with Schelling. Complete their conversation.**

BROOKS: Now, Schelling, what about this hurricane? Tell me about it. What's it called?

SCHELLING: Mabel, and it's _____

BROOKS: Mmm. Are we in any danger from Mabel?

SCHELLING: Oh no, _____

BROOKS: And does everybody agree with you?

SCHELLING: Well, young Wyatt _____

BROOKS: What's his reason for thinking that?

SCHELLING: He _____

BROOKS: We need facts and figures, not feelings.

SCHELLING: Of course _____

BROOKS: So we've nothing to worry about.

SCHELLING: _____

4 **Today, hurricanes are given men's names as well as women's names. Do you agree with that? Do you think it was wrong to use only women's names before? Why?**

5 Which of these words can be used to talk about war and about hurricanes? Can any words be used for both? Write the words under these headings.

War	Hurricanes	Both

attack, base, blow, drown, fierce, flash, flood, gun, helicopter, headquarters, howl, lightning, mud, navy, rebel, rescue, satellite, savage, shelter, soldier, tidal wave, violent, weapon, wind

Now write some sentences to show how the words in your 'Both' box can be used about war and about hurricanes. For example:

In a hurricane the winds are very fierce.
There was fierce fighting during the battle for St Pierre.

6 Do you agree (A) or disagree (D) with these sentences? Explain why.

1 Favel was fighting a war for a good reason.
2 He was right to use the hurricane as a weapon of war.
3 Using a hurricane is worse than using guns and bombs.
4 'War *is* murder.'

7 Is *Wyatt's Hurricane* a good title for this story? Here are some other possible titles. Which do you like best, and why? Can you think of any other titles?

Wyatt and Mabel   Wind and War
A Caribbean Adventure   The Battle for San Fernandez
Wyatt and Julie   The Big Wind

8 Imagine that you were in St Pierre, staying with a San Fernandez family. Write a letter to a friend at home, describing the night of the hurricane. Think about these questions as you write.

• What were you doing when Favel's soldiers banged on the door?
• What did you take with you when you left?
• Did people help each other in the street (carrying small children, helping old people)?
• Did you see anyone die?
• What were you most frightened of – the war, the crowds of people, the soldiers, the hurricane?
• Where did you go?
• What did you do when the hurricane began?
• How did you feel during that night?
• What did you do when it was all over?

9 Complete this poster asking people in other countries for help after the hurricane. What kind of photographs will you choose for your poster? What other things can you do to make people look at the poster?

WE NEED YOUR HELP NOW

Two days ago there was _____. It destroyed _____ and there were _____. Thousands of people have no _____. They need _____. Please send _____.

ABOUT THE AUTHOR

Desmond Bagley (1923–83) was born in England, and began his working life at the age of fourteen. After several different jobs, he went to work in an aircraft factory at the start of the Second World War. When the war ended, he worked his way overland through Europe and North Africa, reaching South Africa in 1951. In Johannesburg he became a journalist and wrote his first published novel, *The Golden Keel*, in 1962. Two years later he returned to England and became a full-time writer.

He wrote fifteen novels, all adventure thrillers, and each one was a bestseller. His stories are usually about groups of people who have to fight to stay alive in difficult, dangerous situations. Sometimes the danger is from accidents or disasters – as in *Wyatt's Hurricane*. Sometimes it is from other people, often spies or criminals. His stories are fast and exciting, and you never know what is going to happen next. In *The Enemy* (also retold in the Oxford Bookworms Library, at Stage 6), for example, you don't find out who 'the enemy' really is until a long way into the novel. Desmond Bagley always has another surprise waiting for the reader.

OXFORD BOOKWORMS LIBRARY

Classics • Crime & Mystery • Factfiles • Fantasy & Horror
Human Interest • Playscripts • Thriller & Adventure
True Stories • World Stories

The OXFORD BOOKWORMS LIBRARY provides enjoyable reading in English, with a wide range of classic and modern fiction, non-fiction, and plays. It includes original and adapted texts in seven carefully graded language stages, which take learners from beginner to advanced level. An overview is given on the next pages.

All Stage 1 titles are available as audio recordings, as well as over eighty other titles from Starter to Stage 6. All Starters and many titles at Stages 1 to 4 are specially recommended for younger learners. Every Bookworm is illustrated, and Starters and Factfiles have full-colour illustrations.

The OXFORD BOOKWORMS LIBRARY also offers extensive support. Each book contains an introduction to the story, notes about the author, a glossary, and activities. Additional resources include tests and worksheets, and answers for these and for the activities in the books. There is advice on running a class library, using audio recordings, and the many ways of using Oxford Bookworms in reading programmes. Resource materials are available on the website <www.oup.com/elt/bookworms>.

The *Oxford Bookworms Collection* is a series for advanced learners. It consists of volumes of short stories by well-known authors, both classic and modern. Texts are not abridged or adapted in any way, but carefully selected to be accessible to the advanced student.

You can find details and a full list of titles in the *Oxford Bookworms Library Catalogue* and *Oxford English Language Teaching Catalogues*, and on the website <www.oup.com/elt/bookworms>.

THE OXFORD BOOKWORMS LIBRARY
GRADING AND SAMPLE EXTRACTS

STARTER • 250 HEADWORDS

present simple – present continuous – imperative –
can/cannot, must – *going to* (future) – simple gerunds …

Her phone is ringing – but where is it?

Sally gets out of bed and looks in her bag. No phone. She looks under the bed. No phone. Then she looks behind the door. There is her phone. Sally picks up her phone and answers it. *Sally's Phone*

STAGE 1 • 400 HEADWORDS

… past simple – coordination with *and*, *but*, *or* –
subordination with *before*, *after*, *when*, *because*, *so* …

I knew him in Persia. He was a famous builder and I worked with him there. For a time I was his friend, but not for long. When he came to Paris, I came after him – I wanted to watch him. He was a very clever, very dangerous man. *The Phantom of the Opera*

STAGE 2 • 700 HEADWORDS

… present perfect – *will* (future) – *(don't) have to, must not, could* –
comparison of adjectives – simple *if* clauses – past continuous –
tag questions – *ask/tell* + infinitive …

While I was writing these words in my diary, I decided what to do. I must try to escape. I shall try to get down the wall outside. The window is high above the ground, but I have to try. I shall take some of the gold with me – if I escape, perhaps it will be helpful later. *Dracula*

STAGE 3 • 1000 HEADWORDS

... should, may – present perfect continuous – *used to* – past perfect –
causative – relative clauses – indirect statements ...

Of course, it was most important that no one should see
Colin, Mary, or Dickon entering the secret garden. So Colin
gave orders to the gardeners that they must all keep away
from that part of the garden in future. ***The Secret Garden***

STAGE 4 • 1400 HEADWORDS

... past perfect continuous – passive (simple forms) –
would conditional clauses – indirect questions –
relatives with *where/when* – gerunds after prepositions/phrases ...

I was glad. Now Hyde could not show his face to the world
again. If he did, every honest man in London would be proud
to report him to the police. ***Dr Jekyll and Mr Hyde***

STAGE 5 • 1800 HEADWORDS

... future continuous – future perfect –
passive (modals, continuous forms) –
would have conditional clauses – modals + perfect infinitive ...

If he had spoken Estella's name, I would have hit him. I was so
angry with him, and so depressed about my future, that I could
not eat the breakfast. Instead I went straight to the old house.
Great Expectations

STAGE 6 • 2500 HEADWORDS

... passive (infinitives, gerunds) – advanced modal meanings –
clauses of concession, condition

When I stepped up to the piano, I was confident. It was as if I
knew that the prodigy side of me really did exist. And when I
started to play, I was so caught up in how lovely I looked that
I didn't worry how I would sound. ***The Joy Luck Club***

BOOKWORMS • THRILLER & ADVENTURE • STAGE 3

Kidnapped

ROBERT LOUIS STEVENSON

Retold by Clare West

'I ran to the side of the ship. "Help, help! Murder!" I screamed, and my uncle slowly turned to look at me. I did not see any more. Already strong hands were pulling me away. Then something hit my head; I saw a great flash of fire, and fell to the ground . . .'

And so begin David Balfour's adventures. He is kidnapped, taken to sea, and meets many dangers. He also meets a friend, Alan Breck. But Alan is in danger himself, on the run from the English army across the wild Highlands of Scotland . . .

BOOKWORMS • CLASSICS • STAGE 3

The Call of the Wild

JACK LONDON

Retold by Nick Bullard

When men find gold in the frozen north of Canada, they need dogs – big, strong dogs to pull the sledges on the long journeys to and from the gold mines.

Buck is stolen from his home in the south and sold as a sledge-dog. He has to learn a new way of life – how to work in harness, how to stay alive in the ice and the snow . . . and how to fight. Because when a dog falls down in a fight, he never gets up again.